WORLD BELIEFS AND CULTURES

Islam

Revised and Updated

Sue Penney

Heinemann Library
Chicago, Illinois

a division of Reed Elsevier Inc.
Chicago, Illinois

Customer Service 888-454-2279
Visit our website at www.heinemannraintree.com

Designed by Steve Mead and Debbie Oatley
Printed and bound in China by Leo Paper Group

12 11 10 09 08
10 9 8 7 6 5 4 3 2 1

New edition ISBNs: 1-4329-0315-2 (hardcover)
1-4329-0322-5 (paperback)
13-digit ISBNs: 978-1-4329-0315-2 (hardcover)
978-1-4329-0322-0 (paperback)

The Library of Congress has cataloged the first edition as follows:
Penney, Sue.
Islam / Sue Penney.
p. cm. -- (World beliefs and cultures)
Includes bibliographical references and index.
Summary: An overview of the beliefs and customs of Islam, including an introduction to sacred texts, a history of the religion, important holidays, and worship practices around the world.
Audience: 5-7
ISBN 1-57572-357-3 (HC), 1-4034-4165-0 (Pbk.)
1. Islam. 2. Islam--Doctrines [1. Islam.] I. Title. II. Series.

BP161.2.P46 2000
297--dc21

00-024007

Acknowledgments
The publishers would like to thank the following for permission to reproduce copyright material: *Roman transliteration of the Holy Qur'an* with English translation, Abdullah Yusuf Ali, Sh Muhammad Ashraf Publishers, Pakistan.

The publishers would like to thank the following for permission to reproduce photographs: Alamy/Sally and Richard Greenhill p. **18**; Ancient Art and Architecture p. **35**; Andes Press Agency/Carlos Reyes-Manzo p. **40**; Circa Photo Library/William Holtby pp. **25**, **31**, **32**, **41**; PA Photos/AP/Nader Daoud p. **38**; Panos Pictures/ Warrick Page p. **37**; Peter Sanders pp. **5**, **6**, **7**, **8**, **11**, **12**, **13**, **14**, **15**, **16**, **17**, **20**, **21**, **22**, **23**, **24**, **26**, **27**, **28**, **29**, **30**, **33**, **34**, **36**, **39**; Photoedit, Inc. pp. **4** (Jeff Greenberg), **19** (A. Ramey), **42** (Bob Daemmrich). Background image on cover and inside book from istockphoto.com/Bart Broek.

Cover photo of Muslims gathering for prayer at the Jama Masjid Mosque, Delhi, reproduced with permission of Alamy/Fredrik Renander.

The publishers would like to thank Mark A. Berkson for his comments in the preparation of this book.

Every effort has been made to contact copyright holders of any material reproduced in this book. Any omissions will be rectified in subsequent printings if notice is given to the publishers.

Contents

Some words are shown in bold, **like this**. You can find out what they mean by looking in the glossary.

Dates: In this book, dates are followed by the letters BCE (Before the Common Era) or CE (Common Era). This is instead of using BC (Before Christ) and AD (*Anno Domini*, meaning "in the year of our Lord"). The date numbers are the same in both systems.

Introducing Islam

Islam is the religion of people called Muslims. The word "Islam" and the word "Muslim" both come from an **Arabic** word that is best translated as "submission." "Submission" means "to place under"—in other words, to accept that someone else is more important than oneself and to obey that person. Muslims believe that they submit to **Allah**. "Allah" is the Arabic word for "God." This submission is an active decision to live according to God's will.

Muslims are part of many different cultures.

What do Muslims believe?

Muslims believe that there is one God—Allah. They believe that Allah is **eternal**. In other words, he was never born and will never die. He has always been there. He is all-powerful and knows everything. He created the universe, the world, and everything in it. He cares about what he made. He created human beings, and they have a duty to worship him in return for all that he has done for them.

Muslims believe that the nonhuman natural world always follows God's law, but that human beings have free will. They are able to choose to submit and be Muslims or to follow a different path. Believing in Allah is not enough. They must live in the right way, too. Muslims call this **niyyah**, meaning "intention." They believe that the intention to live a good life is essential to being a Muslim. This does not mean that they expect everyone to succeed all the time, but it is necessary for people to try as hard as they can. They believe that Allah is merciful and will judge what their intentions were.

Prophets

Muslims believe that Allah chooses people to be **prophets** in order to deliver his message to humanity. Some prophets are messengers who bring a message from Allah in the form of Scripture. Muslims believe that there have been 124,000 prophets over thousands of years, and all of them were Muslims. The first prophet was Adam, the first man. The last propet was a man called Muhammad. He was born in the country we now call Saudi Arabia in the year 570 CE. Muslims believe that Muhammad received messages from Allah, given to him by an angel. These messages were the words of Allah and can never be changed. They were collected together to form the Muslims' holy book, which is called the **Qur'an**.

The Shahadah

The most important beliefs of Islam are summed up in the **Shahadah**. This is also called the Declaration of Faith. In Arabic it is "La ilaha illa-Llah, Muhamad rasulu-Allah." This is usually translated as "There is no God except God [Allah], and Muhammad is the messenger of God [Allah]." These are the first words said to a newborn Muslim baby and the last words said by a Muslim who is dying, if he or she is still able to speak. Among observant Muslims, they are the first words said upon waking up and the last words said before going to sleep. The Shahadah also forms part of the Call to Prayer (see page 23).

This is the Shahadah, made into a picture.

Islam fact check

- Muslims believe that there is only one God. Muslims believe that Allah (the Arabic word for "God") is the same God that is worshiped by Christians and Jews.
- The Muslim place of worship is called a **mosque** ("**masjid**" in Arabic).
- The Muslim holy book is called the Qur'an.
- The Muslim calendar dates from 622 CE. This is when Muhammad moved to Medina, an event called the **Hijra**.
- The symbol most often used for Islam is a crescent moon and a star. No one really knows where this symbol came from, but many people believe it comes from the fact that Islam has its roots in desert countries. People traveled at night when it was cooler and used the moon and stars to guide them, just as their religion guides them through life.
- There are estimated to be 1.3 to 1.5 billion Muslims in the world today, living in almost every country in the world. Scholars roughly estimate that there are around 3 to 6 million Muslims in the United States, about 1.5 million in Great Britain, and about 220,000 in Australia.
- In most of the countries in northern Africa and the Middle East, over half the population is Muslim. South Asia has the world's highest Muslim population, and Indonesia is the country with the most Muslims.
- In Europe, Islam is the second-largest religion after Christianity.

The Life of Muhammad

You can find the places mentioned in this book on the map on page 44.

These traders still live and work in ways similar to Muhammad.

Muhammad was born in the city of Mecca, in the country we now call Saudi Arabia. Muslims believe he was born in the year 570 CE, on the twelfth day of the third month. His mother, Amina, was a widow. According to the local custom, she sent Muhammad to live among the Bedouin for a while. These were a nomadic people (people who did not settle in one place) who lived in the Arabian peninsula. After Amina died, Muhammad was cared for by his grandfather. Two years later his grandfather died, and Muhammad lived with his uncle.

Mecca was an important trading center, and Muhammad's uncle was a trader. From about the age of 12, Muhammad began helping his uncle. By the time he was an adult, Muhammad had become well known for his honesty and goodness. He was given the nickname Al-Amin, which means "the trustworthy one." He began working for a wealthy woman named Khadijah, who was also a trader. When Muhammad was 25, he and Khadijah were married. Muhammad was respected, rich, and happily married. It seemed that his life had everything he could possibly want.

However, Muhammad had always been a thoughtful man, and there were evidently times when he needed to be by himself. He needed to **meditate** about his life and the things that were happening in the world around him. He was unhappy about what he saw in the life of Mecca. There were wealthy people, but many of them spent their days gambling, drinking, and fighting. The rich cheated the poor. The worship of **idols** was common, and it often included **sacrifices**. Muhammad was sure that these things were wrong.

One night, when he was about 40 years old, Muhammad was meditating in a cave on Mount Hira. Muslims believe that he saw the angel Gabriel ("Jibril" in Arabic). Gabriel was a messenger from Allah, giving Muhammad words of **revelation** that he must recite. Muslims believe that this was the first of the revelations of the Qur'an. As Muhammad stood up and walked out of the cave, he heard the angel say, "Muhammad! You are Allah's messenger!"

Muhammad was terrified by this experience. He feared that he might be going mad or that an evil force was trying to make him claim special powers for himself. He returned home and told Khadijah what had happened. She comforted him and went to talk to her cousin, an old man who was a devout Christian and whose judgment she respected. He was sure that Muhammad had indeed seen a messenger from God. Khadijah became the first person to believe in the words that Muhammad spoke.

This is the Great Mosque in Mecca today, with Mount Hira in the background.

Some months later, Muhammad had another revelation. Then, there was a gap of two years before the revelations began again. After this, Muhammad continued to receive messages and instructions from Allah for the rest of his life. For several years, Muhammad did not speak of his experiences, except to his friends and family. Then, the angel told him that he must go out and preach to the people of Mecca. His message was not well received. The people did not like being told that the way they lived was wrong. They made a lot of money from people coming to worship the idols, and they did not want to get rid of them in order to worship only Allah.

After several years, men from the neighboring town of Yathrib heard Muhammad preaching. They were impressed and asked him to go to their town and become a religious leader there. At last, Muhammad agreed. His journey to Yathrib—later called Medina—is called the Hijra.

The Hadith

The most important teachings of Islam are those of the Qur'an, which Muslims believe were Allah's words, given to Muhammad by the angel Gabriel. They also have enormous respect for the **Hadith**, which means "traditions." The Hadith are traditional teachings that go back to the time of Muhammad. There are two sorts of Hadith: the sacred and the prophetic. The sacred Hadith are so called because Muslims believe that they are teachings that came from Allah—although they were not part of the revelations of the Qur'an. The prophetic Hadith are teachings that were given by Muhammad himself, based on experiences in his life. Because Muhammad was an exemplary Muslim, in the sense that his words and deeds were in perfect accordance with God's will, he is considered by many to be the "living Qur'an." That is why Muslims strive to live like Muhammad and to follow his way.

This is the Mosque of the Prophet in Medina today.

The Hijra

You can find the places mentioned in this book on the map on page 44.

Muhammad made the dangerous journey to Yathrib, or Medina, in 622 CE. Yathrib was about 200 miles (320 kilometers) from Mecca. The journey was dangerous because some of the people in Mecca had been unhappy with Muhammad's teachings. They wanted to get rid of him, and in the desert it would be easy to ambush and kill him. There are several stories in the Muslim tradition about how Allah protected Muhammad on the journey. One story says that he was hiding in a cave when his enemies came right to the entrance, but because a spider had built its web and a bird was nesting there, they did not search it.

When Muhammad arrived in Yathrib, he was treated as an honored prophet—a messenger from God. Everyone wanted him to go and stay in their house. To avoid offending anyone, Muhammad said he would let his camel choose where he was going to live. The camel knelt down at a spot where dates were laid out to dry. Muhammad bought the land and built a house there. Later, in part of the same site, he built a place of worship where Muslims could meet for prayer. The site is still preserved and respected by Muslims as being the first mosque in the world.

Muhammad became a religious leader and also the leader of the city. Many people listened to his preaching and began to follow the new religion. It became so popular that the city became known as Madinat-n-Nabi, which means "the City of the Prophet." Later, this name was shortened to Medina, which is the name still used today. The journey to Medina was called the Hijra, which means "emigration." Muslims recognized that this was a very important event, so they began to number the years after it. The years of the Muslim calendar are therefore followed by the letters AH—After the Hijra.

War with Mecca

Muhammad worked in Medina for 10 years, teaching and preaching. The new religion grew and developed as Muhammad shared the instructions that he was receiving from Allah. The people of Mecca were not happy about the fact that the religion was becoming stronger and stronger. They began to cause trouble for Muhammad and his followers. There were many small fights between the two sides, and there were two major battles. The first of these was at Badr in 624 CE and was won by the Muslims. The second was at Uhud in 625 CE, when neither side could claim victory.

Muhammad still wanted to return to Mecca. In 628 CE he received a message from Allah that told him that he would soon return to Mecca in triumph. He went to Mecca with a group of his followers, and the Meccans made a treaty with him that allowed Muslims to travel to Mecca safely. Muhammad returned to Medina. Two years later, the Meccans broke the treaty, and Muhammad set out with an army of 10,000 men.

The people of Mecca surrendered without a fight, and Muhammad claimed the city for Islam. Normally, a victor would take revenge on the conquered people, but Muhammad did not. Before long, everyone in Mecca accepted the new religion. The idols were thrown out of the city and it became a holy city dedicated to Allah. No one who was not a Muslim was allowed to go there. This rule still applies today.

Muhammad returned to Medina and spent the next two years preaching. He died of a fever on Rabi-ul-Awwal 12, 11 AH (June 8, 632 CE; Rabi-ul-Awwal is the name of a month in the Islamic calendar). He was buried where he had died, at the home of his youngest wife, Aisha. The Mosque of the Prophet is built over his tomb.

"Peace be upon him"

Muslims do not regard Muhammad as being the founder of Islam. They believe that their religion was founded by Allah at the creation and that Muhammad was the last of the prophets whom Allah sent to Earth. They respect Muhammad enormously, but they do not worship him. They believe that only Allah should be worshiped. To show their respect, whenever they mention the names of the prophets and of some of the great Muslim leaders, Muslims say, "Alaihi salaam," which means, "Peace be upon him." Whenever they mention the name of Muhammad, Muslims say, "Salla-Allah alaihi wa sallam," which means, "Peace and blessings of Allah upon him." When writing in English, Muslims often use "pbuh" or "saw" (from the first letters of the Arabic words) to shorten the phrases. In Arabic, the language of Islam, these two phrases are written down in a special way, like this:

"Peace be upon him." *"Peace and blessings of Allah upon him."*

The History of Islam

The first caliphs

Muhammad died in 632 CE, and his followers had to decide who would become their new leader. Muhammad and his first wife, Khadijah, had had two sons, but both died in infancy. Many Muslims felt that Muhammad's son-in-law, Ali, should take over the leadership. Other Muslims wanted to hold elections and nominate Abu Bakr as leader. Abu Bakr had been one of Muhammad's closest friends, and he was the father of Muhammad's wife, Aisha. Abu Bakr's supporters won, and Abu Bakr became the new leader.

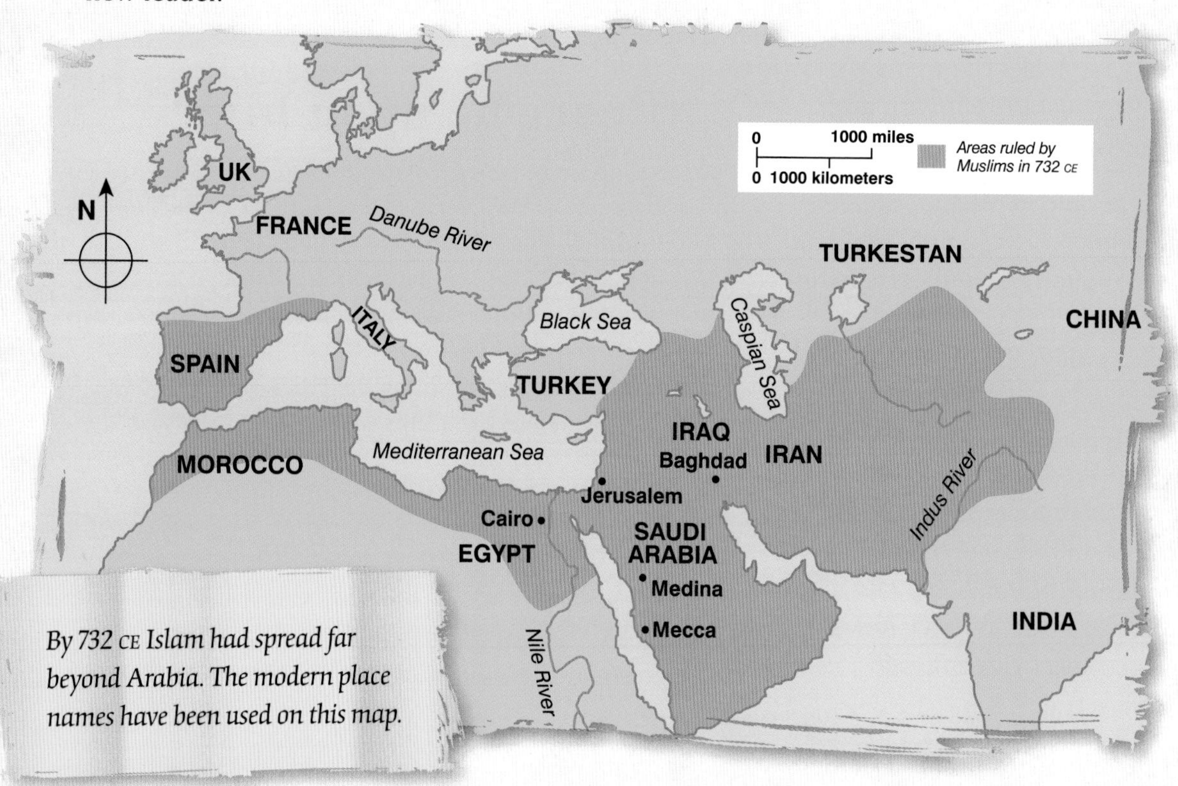

By 732 CE Islam had spread far beyond Arabia. The modern place names have been used on this map.

The leaders were called **caliphs**, which means "successors." Abu Bakr was caliph for two years. During this time, all of Arabia became Muslim, and the religion was spreading into the surrounding countries. He chose Umar, another friend of Muhammad's, to be the next caliph after him. Umar was caliph for 10 years, and in that time Muslim armies conquered Syria and Palestine and began to spread into Egypt and Iran.

In 644 CE Umar was murdered by one of his servants. Umar was succeeded as caliph by Uthman. According to Islamic tradition, during the reign of Uthman, the Qur'an was compiled into its final format. Uthman ruled until 656 CE, when he, too, was murdered. The fourth caliph was Ali, Muhammad's son-in-law, whom some Muslims had wanted to be the first caliph 24 years earlier. He ruled for five years, during which there were two rebellions against him. When he was murdered, the position of caliph passed to his main rival, Muawiya. This led to differences of opinion between Muslims about who was really a caliph and who the next one should be (see pages 12–13).

The spread of Islam

The prayer room in the Great Mosque in Cordoba, Spain, dates from the 8th to 10th centuries CE.

During the time of the first caliphs, Islam spread very quickly. By the time of Muhammad's death, almost all of Arabia had become Muslim, and within 100 years after his death, countries as far as Spain and India were ruled by Muslims.

In 637 CE a Muslim army captured Jerusalem, and by 642 CE Muslims were in control of present-day Egypt. By 700 CE Muslims controlled almost all of the North African coast.

Where the army led, traders soon followed. This was another way in which Islam spread. The traders took their religion with them and became well known for the fact that they lived good lives and were honest to deal with. Many people respected them, and some decided that they wanted to become Muslims, too.

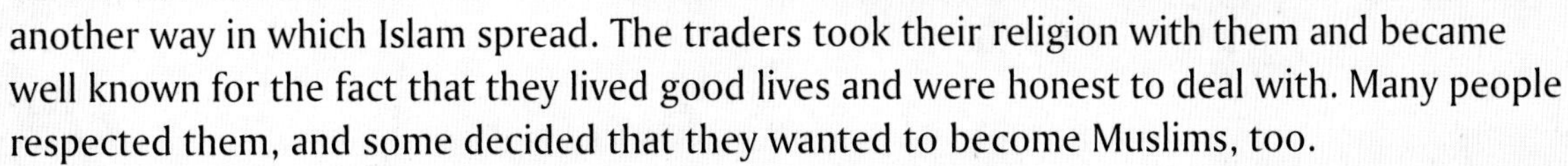

In places where Muslims ruled people who belonged to other religions, those people were generally tolerated as long as they did not interfere with the Muslim way of life. The Qur'an teaches clearly that people cannot be forced to convert to Islam. Non-Muslims had to pay a special tax, but those who became Muslims lived tax-free.

Jihad

"**Jihad**" means "striving," or trying to live and do everything for the love of Allah. Jihad is a struggle against the elements within oneself—for example, greed or selfishness—that provide challenges to following God's law. For most Muslims, this means prayer or giving extra money to charity—any effort people make to serve Allah to the best of their ability. This is "major jihad." Sometimes the word "jihad" is used to apply to a war-like situation and is translated as "holy war." This is "minor jihad." Holy wars can only be fought in defense, never as the aggressor, and there are strict rules about the way in which the war must be fought.

Branches of Islam

For 24 years after the death of Muhammad, there were differences of opinion among Muslims about who should be the caliph. Then, after the murder of Ali, Muawiya became the leader. He was a member of the Umayyad family, who were the most important tribe in Mecca. This caused another problem. Many Muslims did not want to be led by a member of the family that had been responsible for persecuting Muslims in Mecca. They claimed that the position of caliph should stay in Muhammad's family, and now that Ali was dead, the next caliph should be his son, Hasan.

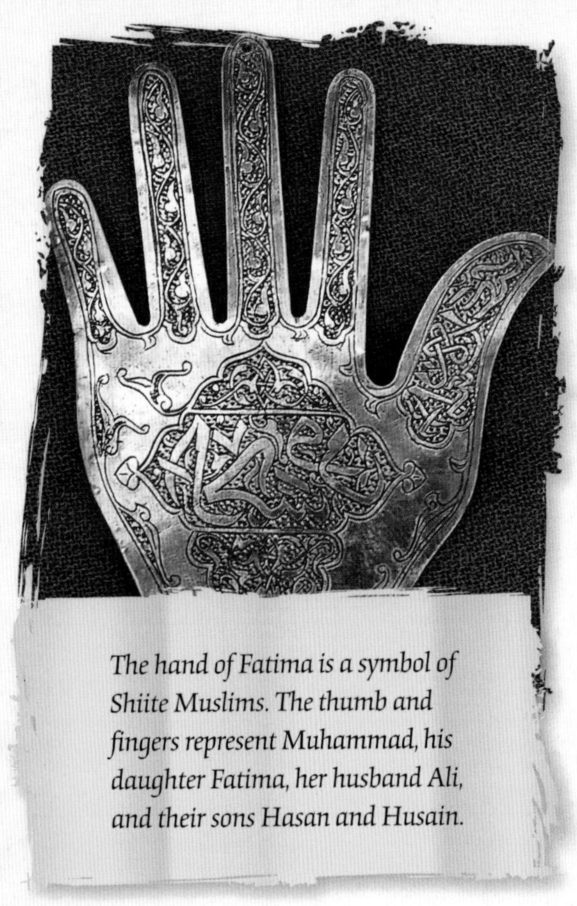

The hand of Fatima is a symbol of Shiite Muslims. The thumb and fingers represent Muhammad, his daughter Fatima, her husband Ali, and their sons Hasan and Husain.

The political differences of opinion led to two branches of Islam developing. Those who supported Ali became known as the Shi'ah Ali, which means the "Party of Ali." They are now known as Shiites or Shia Muslims. The other group took the name Sunni, from the word "sunnah," which means "example." They believe that they are the people who follow the line of authority from Muhammad. Both groups follow all the teachings of Islam.

Sunni Muslims

About 85 percent of Muslims today belong to the group called Sunnis. They believe that Muhammad intended the leader of the Muslims to be chosen by the community leaders. This would mean that the best person could be chosen, rather than that leadership should automatically go to the son of the previous leader. They believe that the Qur'an and the Hadith show the way that Muslims should live.

Shiite Muslims

About 15 percent of Muslims today are Shiites, but that number is increasing. Shiites do not accept the first three caliphs. They say that Ali was the first true **imam** (see page 13). Shiites are totally dedicated to their leaders and follow them with a loyalty that other people sometimes find hard to understand. Shiite teachings emphasize the importance of being willing to give up one's own life for the cause of justice and righteousness.

This belief comes partly from their beliefs about martyrs. Islam teaches that a martyr—someone who dies for what he or she believes—will go straight to Allah and live in **Paradise**. In Islamic teachings, Paradise is often described as a garden of happiness for life after death. Believing this means that some Muslims feel that giving up their life for their beliefs is a price well worth paying because their reward will be so great.

These Shiite Muslims are taking part in the festival of Ashura.

Imams

Those who lead prayer and deliver sermons in mosques are called imams, but the title has a special meaning for Shiite Muslims. Shiites believe that there were twelve imams (some Shiites say seven) who were given special powers by Allah, just as Muhammad was. They believe that the first imam was Ali, whose power passed to his son, and so on. The last imam did not die, but disappeared mysteriously in 880 CE. They believe that one day he will return and bring about an age of justice and righteousness. Until he does, the teaching of the imams is in the hands of "Doctors of the Law" called **Ayatollahs**. In 1979 the Ayatollah Khomeini removed the leader of Iran from power and set up a religious state. Shiite Islam is now the state religion in Iran.

The festival of Ashura

In the month of Muharram every year, Shiite Muslims take part in a festival at Karbala, where the body of Husain, one of Muhammad's grandsons, is buried. Husain was killed in battle in 680 CE, fighting for the position of caliph. Shiite Muslims remember this as a time when evil (the victorious Yazid) triumphed over good (the defeated Husain). During the festival, people remember the dreadful deaths of Husain and his family. There are daily gatherings where emotions are stirred up until most people are weeping, and they all promise to live their lives to ensure that evil cannot triumph again. There are processions and plays showing the events of the battle and the **martyrdoms**. Sometimes men in the processions gash themselves with knives and beat themselves with chains as a way of remembering what Husain suffered.

The Qur'an

There are different versions of the story of the revelation to Muhammad. According to one version, the first revelation of the Qur'an came when Muhammad was meditating in a cave on Mount Hira, just outside Mecca. Muslims believe he saw an angel who came toward him, carrying a roll of silk on which words were written in fiery letters. The angel said, "Iqra!" which means, "Recite!" Like many people in those days, Muhammad could not read or write, and he said that he could not read the words. The angel repeated the command three times, and each time Muhammad said that he could not do so. He said afterward that he felt a pressure building up inside him and something gripping his chest and his throat so tightly that he felt he was going to die. Then, he found that he was able to read the words:

Recite!
In the name of your Lord,
Who created all humanity out of a single drop of blood!
Speak these words aloud!
Your Lord is the Most Generous One,
He who taught the use of the Pen, taught man that which he did not know.
(Sura 96:1–5)

This boy is visiting Jebel Nur, the cave where Muhammad had his first revelation.

The angel identified himself as Gabriel and told Muhammad that he was to be Allah's messenger. Some months later, Muhammad had another **vision**. The angel appeared to him as a huge pair of eyes staring at him and became an enormous figure whose feet touched the horizon. Whichever way he turned, Muhammad could still see the figure. Again, he was terrified.

For the rest of his life, Muhammad continued to receive messages from God. A few times, he saw the angel again. Most times, the messages came as voices in his head. There is a tradition that sometimes he could hear the voices perfectly, but at other times they were muffled.

Muhammad's visions

Muslim tradition says that Muhammad always knew when the visions were going to happen. So, he would lie down, usually wrapped in the cloak that he used as blanket. He sometimes appeared very hot, even in cold weather, and would sweat a great deal.

He often seemed to become unconscious. The visions always made him feel that he was close to death. When the visions came to an end, he would sit up, his normal self again, and repeat what he had been told. It was the duty of his friends as well as of Muhammad himself to memorize the words, so that none of the message was lost.

This handwritten copy of the Qur'an is over 200 years old.

What Muslims believe about the Qur'an

Muslims believe that the Qur'an is made up of the direct words of Allah, given to human beings through the "mouthpiece" of Muhammad. Muslims respect the teachings that Muhammad gave himself, but they are in a different class from the words of the Qur'an, which came from Allah and can never be changed. This is why they believe that the actual words of the Qur'an are so important. However, there are different ways to understand its meaning. Some Muslims follow a literal interpretation of the Qur'an, while others see things in a more symbolic way.

Muslims do not believe that Muhammad was the first person to receive a revelation from Allah. However, they believe that the revelations given to other people (for example, the Torah of the Jews or the Gospels of the Christians) have been changed by the people who wrote them down and by subsequent generations. They can no longer be relied upon to represent perfectly the words of Allah.

Translations

Arabic is the language of the Qur'an. It uses letters that are very different from the Roman letters used in English and most European languages. This means that an Arabic word needs to be transliterated, or changed into another alphabet, as well as translated, or giving its meaning. There are no exact equivalents to the sound of Arabic letters in the Roman alphabet. This means that the letters that give the sound nearest to the original have to be used. Opinions have changed about which letters should be used, and this is why many Arabic words have more than one spelling in the Roman alphabet. For example, Muhammad's name can be spelled Mohamed, Mohammad, and Mahomet. Mecca is often spelled Makkah. The differences are not wrong—they are just alternatives.

A beautifully decorated copy of the Qur'an is open at the first two suras.

Suras

The Qur'an is made up of chapters called suras. There are 114 suras altogether, which are of different lengths. The longest is sura 2, which has 286 verses. The shortest is sura 103, which has only three verses. Except for one (sura 9), the suras all begin with the words "In the name of Allah, the gracious, the merciful." The suras are not in the order that the words were received by Muhammad. Muslims believe that not long before he died, Muhammad received instructions about the order in which they were to be kept.

Muslims believe that the words of the Qur'an must be preserved exactly as they were given. Muhammad ensured that this happened by repeating all the revelations to his friends and family, who all learned them by heart. In those days, not many people could read or write, and learning things like this was the usual way in which important words were remembered. Islamic tradition states that the complete Qur'an was written down within 20 years of Muhammad's death and has never been altered.

Hafiz

Muslims believe that the Qur'an is the most important book that has ever existed because it contains the words of Allah. To help to ensure that it can never be changed in any way, and because they believe it is so important, many Muslims learn it completely by heart. People who have done this are allowed to use the title **hafiz** as part of their name. They are very respected by other Muslims.

Translations

The Qur'an has been translated into over 40 other languages, but for worship it is only ever used in Arabic. This is because Muslims believe that the translations can never give the exact sense of Allah's words. Even Muslims who do not speak Arabic know some of the words of the Qur'an in the original language and use it for worship.

What does the Qur'an say?

The suras that Muhammad received first are about the oneness of Allah, Muhammad's role as a prophet, and what will happen at the Last Judgment. Later suras are about everyday matters such as marriage, the law, and how to live as a Muslim. The suras are labeled as Meccan or Medinan suras, based on where they were received.

Quotes from the Qur'an

Forbidden to you for food
Are: carrion, blood,
the flesh of swine, and that
On which has been invoked
The name other than the name of Allah.
That which has been killed by strangling
or by a violent blow,
Or by a headlong fall . . . (Sura 5: 3)

Those who patiently persevere,
And seek their Lord with regular prayers,
and give generously,
These overcome evil with good.
For them there is
the final attainment of the
Eternal home. (Sura 13: 22)

He is God,
the one the most unique,
God the immanently indispensable.
He has begotten no one
and is begotten of none.
There is no one comparable to Him.
(Sura 112)

Surely the believers [Muslims]
and the Jews, Nazareans [Christians]
and the Sabians, whoever believes in God
and the Last Day, and whosoever does
right, shall have his reward with the Lord
and will neither have fear nor regret.
(Sura 2: 62)

Muslims believe that learning to read the Qur'an is very important.

How to treat the Qur'an

Muslims treat the Qur'an with enormous respect. While it is being read, they do not eat, drink, or speak. They do not touch it unnecessarily. While it is being read, it is often placed on a special stool called a **kursi**. It is never allowed to touch the ground. Before beginning to read the Qur'an, Muslims wash their hands, and if they are at all dirty, they will bath completely. A woman is not permitted to touch it while she is menstruating. When it is not in use, it is kept on a high shelf, and nothing is ever placed on top of it. It is covered to protect it from dust and damage.

Ways of Worship

A family reads the Qur'an at home.

Observant Muslims believe that their religion affects everything they do, because they have submitted their lives to Allah. This means that their home is the center of their faith.

Decorations

Most Muslim families have pictures on the walls that are connected with their religion. These are always placed high up as a sign of respect. There may be pictures of important mosques, or of the **Kaaba**, the most important **shrine** in Mecca. Pictures of people are never use because Muhammad said they were not allowed in case people began to worship them. Of course, most Muslims have ordinary photographs of friends and family because these are not used as part of the religion.

The five pillars of Islam

The five pillars are the foundation of Muslim worship and beliefs. They are called pillars because they support the religion in the same way that a pillar supports a building. Muslims believe that believing in and keeping the five pillars helps them to follow their religion properly.

- The first pillar is the **Shahadah**, the Declaration of Faith.
- The second pillar is **Salat**, prayer five times a day.
- The third pillar is **Zakat**, which means "giving to charity."
- The fourth pillar is **Sawm**, which means "**fasting**." Every year, Muslims fast during the hours of daylight for the month of **Ramadan**.
- The fifth pillar is **Hajj**. This is the **pilgrimage** to Mecca, which every Muslim tries to make at least once in his or her lifetime.

The Qur'an

Reading the Qur'an at home together is a part of everyday life in many Muslim families. For women, who do not go to the mosque as often as the men, it is especially important. Children are brought up to read the Qur'an at home and to treat it with great respect.

Food

Muslims believe that all food comes from God and should be treated accordingly. Like many religions, there are restrictions about what foods should and should not be eaten. For Muslims, these restrictions come from the Qur'an. Food that Muslims can eat is *halal*, or permitted. Food that they cannot eat is *haram*, or forbidden. Muslims are allowed to eat all fruits, grains, and vegetables. They can eat fish, poultry, sheep, goats, and camels, but anything that comes from a pig is strictly forbidden.

Keeping the rules about halal foods is an important part of being a Muslim.

For an animal product to be *halal*, the animal must have been killed by the *halal* method. The jugular artery in the neck is severed by a razor-sharp knife. Muslims believe that this is the kindest method of killing an animal. The knife is so sharp that the animal does not feel pain and is unconscious before it has time to suffer. The blood drains away, so the meat does not contain any blood, which would make it *haram*. While the knife is being used, the person using it must repeat the name of Allah. This shows that the animal is not being killed thoughtlessly, and that the life is being returned to Allah, who gave it. Avoiding non-*halal* animals does not just mean avoiding the meat. Many other foods contain animal products, so all ingredients have to be checked.

Alcohol and tobacco

Muslims are expected not to drink alcohol. Alcohol creates intoxication, which can distract a person from prayer and other obligations. In some Muslim countries, the possession of alcohol is against the law. Many Muslims try to avoid being anywhere where alcohol is being served or drunk. In particular, Muslims should not mention Allah or the Qur'an when they are anywhere near alcohol. The use of nonmedical drugs is also forbidden. Smoking is forbidden by some religious authorities and discouraged by others because of its harmful effects.

Daily prayers

Muslims believe that they can pray anywhere and at any time. Five times a day, however, they make special prayers called Salat. These times are between first light and sunrise, after the sun has left its highest point, between mid-afternoon and sunset, between sunset and dark, and between darkness and dawn. Muslims do not pray at dawn, noon, or sunset, because they believe that this would be like pagan sun-worship.

Praying at these times involves putting everything else to one side and concentrating on Allah. To do this requires preparation and discipline. Many Muslim men go to the mosque for prayers as often as they can. The most important prayers, which all adult males are expected to attend, are the second prayers of the day on a Friday. Women may attend the mosque, and if they do not, they are expected to pray at home. Children are expected to practice Salat from about the age of seven. By the age of twelve, it is a religious duty.

Men engage in Wudu in India.

A Muslim may pray in any clean place, and a special mat is often used. As part of the preparation, the body and clothes should be clean, and the worshiper should be dressed appropriately. A man should be dressed modestly. A woman's entire body should be covered except for her face and hands. She should not wear makeup and perfume. Like everything else in a Muslim's life, it is the niyyah—intention—that is most important. All the external actions of prayer are no use if the worshiper does not have the right attitude.

Wudu

Wudu is the special washing before prayer. It puts a person in a state of purity before coming before Allah. Washing off pollutants, such as dirt or sweat, helps people achieve this purity. It also forms a break from what they were doing and gives them time to get ready to concentrate on their prayers. Some Muslims prefer to use cold water, so that they are more alert—especially for the first prayers in the morning!

Washing is always done in the same order, to make sure that nothing is forgotten. The instructions for how it should be done are in the Qur'an. First, the right hand is washed to the wrist. Then, the left hand is washed in the same way. Next, the mouth and throat are washed by gargling, so that the voice is clean to talk to Allah.

Then, the nose and face are washed, then the right arm up to the elbow, then the left. The head is wiped with a wet hand, then the ears are cleaned. Finally, the feet are washed up to the ankles, right one first. If no water is available, people may touch clean earth or sand and then go through the motions of washing. After washing, they cover their head and face the direction of Mecca before they begin to pray.

Rak'ahs

Salat consists of set prayers that are repeated each time. Each repetition is connected with a sequence of movements called a **rak'ah**. Two rak'ahs are made at morning prayers, four at midday and in the afternoon, three in the evening, and four at night.

There are eight positions in a rak'ah. The first is when Muslims stand to attention, showing that they intend to pray. Then, they bow, stand, kneel, and, in the humblest position of all, **prostrate** to touch the ground with the forehead, nose, palms of both hands, knees, and toes. This position shows that they love God more than they love themselves. Then, they kneel again, and then prostrate again. The last movement of a rak'ah is to turn the head from side to side to greet the other people worshiping and the two angels that Muslims believe are always with every person. At the end of a rak'ah, Muslims may finish praying or add private prayers of their own, which are called **du'a**.

These are the first words of the Qur'an, said by Muslims while they are in the second prayer position:

All praise be to Allah, the Lord of the Universe, the most merciful, the most kind, Master of the **Day of Judgment***.*
You alone do we worship,
From you alone do we seek help.
Show us the next step along the straight path of those earning your favor.
Keep us from the path of those earning your anger, those who are going astray.
(Sura 1)

These men sit in the last position of a rak'ah.

Mosques

You can find the places mentioned in this book on the map on page 44.

Muslims believe that they can worship Allah in any clean place, but like people of many religions, they prefer to have a special building where they can meet for worship. This building is called a mosque, or masjid (the Arabic name). "Masjid" means "a place where people prostrate themselves"—in other words, where they bow down to worship.

There are thousands of mosques all over the world, because a Muslim community will try to build a mosque as soon as it can. Islamic law requires a mosque as soon as there are 40 adult male Muslims in any one place. Some mosques are enormous, built to accommodate thousands of worshipers. Others may be tiny. Some are in buildings originally built for other purposes, but used by Muslims for worship. A mosque does not have to be a building. Any place used for the worship of Allah becomes a mosque, so in hot countries a mosque may be outdoors. A piece of sand marked with the direction of Mecca, and perhaps with a mat on the floor, is just as much a mosque as a beautiful building. In many Muslim countries, railroad stations have an arrow on the wall, so that travelers know at once which direction to face for prayers. Many Muslims set aside a room or part of a room that they always use for prayer when they are at home.

This open-air mosque is in Jerusalem.

Other uses for a mosque

Mosques are not only used as a place for prayer. They are used as schools, where children and adults can learn Arabic and study the Qur'an. From the age of four, some children attend **madrassas** (the Arabic word for "school") to learn Arabic and be taught the Qur'an. Part of the mosque may function as a law court, where matters of Islamic law can be decided. Rooms at the mosque may be used for celebrations connected with the religion—for example, birth, marriage, or funeral gatherings. They are used as community centers, where people can meet and discuss matters that affect them in their everyday lives. This is particularly important when Muslims are living in a country in which most other people do not share their faith.

An essential part of all mosques is a water supply. In the past, this was usually a fountain or just a faucet in a courtyard outside the mosque. In many older mosques, this is still the case. Modern mosques usually have washrooms with rows of faucets. It is where Muslims perform wudu—the washing before prayer. Men and women perform this washing separately. There is usually a separate room for women to pray, too. If the mosque is not big enough for this, women pray away from the men. This is to ensure that both groups can concentrate on Allah.

When a mosque has been specially built, it usually has a dome and at least one tall tower called a **minaret**. The dome helps to create a feeling of space inside the mosque and helps the voice of the imam to be heard when the mosque is full of worshipers. The top of the minaret is where the **muezzin** traditionally stands.

The muezzin

Every mosque has a muezzin, whose job it is to call the people to prayer five times a day. The Call to Prayer is called the **adhan**. Some muezzins still chant the adhan from the minaret tower. But in many mosques in towns and cities there is now a loudspeaker system, which allows the adhan to be heard more clearly. It also saves the muezzin the climb to the top of the tower!

The Call to Prayer

The adhan begins with the words "Allahu-Akbar." In English, it translates like this:

God is most great,
God is most great,
God is most great,
God is most great,
I bear witness that
there is no god but Allah,
I bear witness that
there is no god but Allah,
I bear witness that
Muhammad is a messenger of Allah,
I bear witness that
Muhammad is a messenger of Allah,
Come to prayer,
Come to prayer,
Come to flourishing,
Come to flourishing,
God is most great,
God is most great,
There is no god but Allah.

When the muezzin makes the call for the first prayer of the day, he also includes the words "Prayer is better than sleep!"

A U.S. Muslim makes the Call to Prayer.

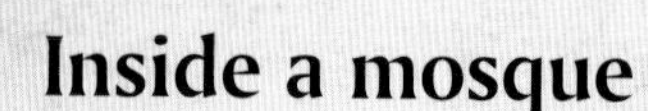

Inside a mosque

Muslims take off their shoes before they enter a mosque. This ensures that it is kept clean for prayer. In most mosques there are shoe racks outside the door. In some large mosques, people keep their shoes with them in a bag. This avoids having to find them among thousands of other pairs at the end of the service. After they have removed their shoes, they perform wudu—washing to make themselves fit for prayer.

Near the entrance of a mosque there may be a bulletin board that can be used to let worshipers know about things that may interest them. There may also be a row of clocks that show the prayer times for that day. These will vary depending on the country and the season, because they take place according to the position of the sun.

There is no furniture in the main room of a mosque. This always makes it seem large and spacious. The floor is usually covered with carpets. Sometimes there is a design on the carpet. Individual mats may be used, with designs of Mecca or a famous mosque. Both the patterned carpet and the mats are intended to help the worshipers make neat rows and face in the right direction. No one has a particular place because everyone is equal in front of Allah. So, it does not matter whether someone is at the back or the front.

The mihrab

In every mosque there is an alcove or arch set into one wall, which shows the **qiblah**, the direction of Mecca. This is called the **mihrab**. It is often very beautifully decorated. It may have tiles and texts from the Qur'an written into it. The prayer leader usually stands in front of the mihrab.

You can find the places mentioned in this book on the map on page 44.

The mimbar

At the front of the mosque, usually at the right-hand side of the mihrab, is the **mimbar**. This is a raised platform where the imam stands when he gives the address at prayers. Some mimbars are very decorated, while others may be just a simple platform or a flight of stairs. The idea is to raise the imam so that everyone in the mosque can see and hear him clearly.

This is the mihrab in the Mosque of the Prophet, Medina.

Decorations

There are never any pictures in a mosque. Muhammad said that they must not be used because there was a danger that people might begin to worship them. (Muslims regard any pictures of Allah or holy beings as blasphemy; in other words, they are insulting to Allah.) Instead of pictures, the mosque is beautifully decorated. The carpets are often made in rich colors with patterns on them. Green is popular because it was Muhammad's favorite color, and a rich turquoise blue is often used, too. The walls may have tiles or other paintings to make them beautiful. These may be pictures of flowers or plants or geometric patterns. Marble pillars and dangling glass chandeliers are other ways in which a mosque can be made to look special.

This calligraphy is part of the decoration in a mosque in Iran.

Calligraphy

A special form of decoration is Islamic **calligraphy**. Calligraphy is the art of beautiful handwriting, especially the art of making writing into pictures. It began when people began to write out verses from the Qur'an. They wanted to make them as beautiful as possible, to show how much they valued them. At first, the words were written on paper or parchment (a material made of animal skin), using sharpened reeds dipped in ink. Later, tiles and pottery began to be decorated in this way, too. Pictures can be made using letters, phrases from the Qur'an, or prayers. In the mosque, these can help the people to worship.

Musa's view

Musa is 12 and lives with his family in London.

I go to the madrassa for **Islamiat** [the study of Islam] on Saturdays, and usually for a couple of hours after school, so that I can learn Arabic and the Qur'an. Sometimes if I've had a hard day at school, it feels like doing extra work, but it's totally different from the way we work at school. I know some of the Qur'an by heart now, and the more I learn Arabic, the easier it is to understand. The imam who teaches us really tries hard to make us understand, and I enjoy feeling that I'm learning more about something that's so important.

The Kaaba

You can find the places mentioned in this book on the map on page 44.

The Kaaba is the most important building in the world for Muslims. It is Islam's holiest shrine. It stands in the central courtyard of the Great Mosque, in the center of Mecca. It was already very old when Muhammad was alive, and no one really knows where it came from. There are two stories. One says that it was built by Adam, the first man, as the first place in the world to worship Allah. Then, it was rebuilt by the prophet Abraham and his son Ishmael to thank Allah for saving Ishmael's life (see page 33). The other tradition says that it was built first by Abraham and Ishmael. Both accounts agree that it was built to worship Allah.

At the time of Muhammad, the Kaaba was a center of worship—but the worship of idols. It contained over 360 statues and altars for worshiping many different gods. Many people came to worship these idols. This was one of the reasons why Mecca was an important center of pilgrimage and such a rich city at the time of Muhammad. After Muhammad had converted the Meccans to Islam, all the idols were thrown out of the city, and the Kaaba became a center of worship for Allah. Ever since, it has been the shrine that all Muslims face when they pray.

The Kaaba is built of brick and is cube-shaped. "Kaaba" means "cube." It measures 49 feet (15 meters) long by 33 feet (10 meters) wide and 46 feet (14 meters) high. Inside it is a room with walls that are covered with quotations from the Qur'an. It is a rare and special privilege for a Muslim to be allowed to pray inside the Kaaba. He can pray and—for the only time in his life—face alternately in all four directions as he prays.

The Black Stone sits in the Kaaba.

During the time of the Hajj, the Kaaba is covered with a black cloth beautifully decorated with the words of the Qur'an in gold embroidery. At the end of Hajj, the cloth is cut into small pieces, and pilgrims are able to take these home with them.

The Black Stone

In one corner of the Kaaba is the Black Stone. This is an oval stone about 7 inches (18 centimeters) long that is probably a meteorite. Today, it is set in silver. It was very old at the time of Muhammad, and there are many stories about it. One story says that Adam found it in the desert when it was gleaming white, but the sins of human beings have caused it to turn black. Another story says that angels took it to heaven for safekeeping at the time of the Great Flood and returned it when Abraham and Ishmael rebuilt the Kaaba.

This shows inside the Mosque of the Dome of the Rock in Jerusalem.

The Mosque of the Prophet

The Mosque of the Prophet is in Medina and was built over the place where Muhammad's body was buried. Muhammad's tomb lies beneath a green dome, and the mosque has been extended and enlarged several times since his death. The mosque also contains the graves of the caliphs Abu Bakr and Umar. It is an important place of pilgrimage for Muslims, especially when they have been on Hajj to Mecca.

The Mosque of the Dome of the Rock

The Mosque of the Dome of the Rock is in Jerusalem. It was built in the 7th century CE and was restored in the 16th century. Jerusalem is the third holiest city for Muslims, after Mecca and Medina. They believe that this mosque marks the place where Muhammad was taken to heaven on the Night of the Journey (see page 35). They also believe that the rock on which this mosque is built is the place where the call to judgment will be sounded on the Day of Judgment.

Muhammad and the Black Stone

When Muhammad was a young man, the Kaaba was being repaired, and the Black Stone had been removed. When it was due to be replaced, an argument broke out among the different tribes in Mecca over who should be given the honor of carrying it. Muhammad settled the argument by spreading a rug on the ground and lifting the Black Stone onto it. The heads of the tribes then took a corner of the rug each, so that they could all carry it. Muslims say that it was because of incidents like these that Muhammad was so respected, even before he began to have revelations from Allah.

Hajj—Pilgrimage to Mecca

Every Muslim who is healthy and who can afford it is expected to go on a pilgrimage to Mecca at least once. To be a true Hajj, the pilgrimage must take place between Zulhijjah 8 and 13, which falls in the last month of the Muslim year. Every year, about two million pilgrims go to Mecca at this time. Pilgrimage at other times of the year is called **Umrah** and is not considered as important.

Pilgrims on Hajj wear special clothes called ihram.

Ihram

While they are on Hajj, pilgrims are expected to live in a special way called **ihram**. They should not swear or argue. Any intimate contact is forbidden, even if husbands and wives are traveling together. To show that the thoughts of all pilgrims are pure, women do not cover their faces, even if they normally do so. No one wears jewelry or cosmetics or uses scented soap. Pilgrims do not cut their hair or trim their nails.

The special clothes for Hajj are also called ihram. Every man wears two white sheets without seams, one wrapped around the lower body and the other draped over the left shoulder. They do not cover their heads, though they may carry an umbrella as protection against the sun. Women wear a plain dress with long sleeves, leaving only their face and hands uncovered. All pilgrims go barefoot or in open sandals. Everyone dresses in the same way, so that there are no distinctions between rich and poor. Everyone is equal before Allah.

Performing Hajj

As soon as pilgrims arrive in Mecca, they hurry to the Kaaba and circle it seven times. They walk quickly, running if possible. Those close enough touch or kiss the Black Stone. Those further away raise their hands toward it. Then, they go to pray near Maqam Abraham (Abraham's place). They hurry seven times between two small hills not far from the Kaaba. Today, the hills are linked by a broad corridor. This reminds pilgrims how Hagar, the handmaiden of Abraham's wife, ran between the two hills desperately looking for water for her son Ishmael. The well they believe Hagar found is called the Well of Zamzam, in the courtyard of the Great Mosque. Pilgrims drink from it and often collect some water to take home for friends and family.

You can find the places mentioned in this book on the map on page 44.

Wuquf

On Zulhijjah 9, the pilgrims travel to the Plain of Arafat, about 12 miles (20 kilometers) from Mecca. Here, they take part in the "stand before Allah," called **wuquf**. This is the most important part of the pilgrimage. They stand from midday to sunset, thinking about Allah and asking him to forgive all the wrong things they have done in their lives. Muslims believe that if it is properly performed, wuquf means that all a person's sins are forgiven. The pilgrims return to Muzdalifah for the evening prayers and to camp overnight.

The Plain of Arafat is crowded during Hajj.

On the morning of Zulhijjah 10, the pilgrims go to Mina, where there are three stone pillars. They throw stones at these, as a reminder of how Abraham drove away the devil who was tempting him. After the first pillar has been stoned, pilgrims sacrifice a sheep or a goat. This is part of the festival of Id-ul-Adha, in which Muslims all over the world take part. Male pilgrims then either cut their hair or shave their heads, and women cut off a lock of their hair. They do this because it is what Muhammad did. They take off their special pilgrim clothes and return to their normal clothes. They camp at Mina for three more days and then travel back to Mecca for a last walk around the Kaaba. They drink as much as they can from the Well of Zamzam, and then the Hajj is ended. Some pilgrims return home, while others stay to visit other holy sites in the area.

Hussain's view

Hussain is 14 and lives in Lahore, Pakistan.

My uncle went on Hajj a couple of years ago. It's so popular now you have to apply for a place. The whole family helped him get ready, making sure he didn't forget anything. In a lot of families, I know people put their money together to get the money to send one person. We couldn't wait for him to come home and tell us all about it. I just can't imagine that many people all gathered together. He said that it's safer now than it used to be, but in the old days people sometimes used to be crushed to death in the crowd. He brought us a bottle of water from the Well of Zamzam. We looked at his ihram clothes, which he brought home so that when he dies he can be buried in them. He said the whole Hajj was a wonderful experience and not like anything else in the whole of his life. I really look forward to the day when I can go.

Celebrations

There are many festivals in the Islamic calendar. One of the most important is **Ramadan**, which is the ninth month of the Muslim calendar. Every year, for the 29 or 30 days of this month, Muslims fast during the hours of daylight. The instruction to perform the fast comes from the Qur'an, and the observance of it goes back to the days of Muhammad.

All eating finishes before dawn, so the day starts well before this. To avoid confusion, lists are published in different places announcing the time when fasting must begin and end. Breakfast is usually a high-energy meal to give a good start to the day. At sunset, there is a light snack, followed by a main meal later.

A family gives thanks before breaking the fast during Ramadan.

Why do Muslims fast?

Muhammad taught his followers that fasting is very important because it is a sign that they have submitted to Allah. It shows that Allah is the most important thing in their life—far more important than food and drink. It is also a great "leveler." Fasting reminds the rich what hunger is like and helps them remember to be compassionate to the poor.

The Muslim calendar

Islam follows a lunar year. This means that each new month begins on the night of the new moon. A month therefore lasts 29 or 30 days, so is slightly shorter than the Western calendar months. This means that each year is about 10 days shorter than a Western year. The months move back through the seasons, year by year, so that over several years each month will have occurred in every season. This is particularly important for celebrations like Ramadan, which involve fasting during daylight hours. Away from the equator, days vary in length throughout the year, so the time of fasting is a great deal longer in July than in January.

Muslims pray at a mosque in Pakistan during Ramadan.

Who fasts?

Eating and drinking nothing all day is very difficult, especially in hot countries. In the United States and Europe, it is not so hot, but the days can be far longer. Muslims believe that Ramadan is intended to be hard but not cruel, so some groups of people are excused from fasting. The very old and the very young are not expected to fast at all. Children from about the age of seven will begin to fast, but they are not expected to fast for the whole month until they are about twelve. People who are sick, or women who are pregnant, are not expected to fast. People traveling are not expected to fast, but should make up for missed days when they return home. If people's health prevents them from fasting—for example, fasting could be fatal for a diabetic—they are expected to pay a sum of money that would buy a meal for 60 people instead. If people break the fast without a good reason, they should fast for an extra 60 days to make it up.

What happens if Muslims do not fast?

There are no punishments if Muslims do not fast. Muslims believe that the judge of someone's behavior is Allah, who knows and sees everything. At the end of the world, everyone will get what they deserve, according to how they have lived. To cheat on the fast is cheating yourself and cheating Allah. Muhammad taught that there are two rewards for everyone who fasts. One is knowing that you have fasted successfully, with the joy of eating again afterward. The other is the reward that you will be given by Allah on the Day of Judgment.

How to live during Ramadan

Ramadan is called the holy month, and Muslims try to live especially pure lives during this month. Muslims who smoke try not to, and they do not have any intimate relations during the day. They spend more time reading the Qur'an and try to spend extra time on religious matters. Many Muslims try to read through the whole Qur'an during the month. During the last 10 days of Ramadan, some Muslims go on a **retreat** to the mosque. They take only basic necessities with them and live as simply as possible, reading the Qur'an and thinking about their religion. This was how Muhammad spent the last 10 days of Ramadan. The festival of Id-ul-Fitr marks the end of Ramadan.

New clothes for Id help to make the festival special.

Id-ul-Fitr

"Id," sometimes spelled "Eid," is the Muslim word for "festival." Id-ul-Fitr is the festival that ends Ramadan, the month when Muslims fast. Before the festival begins, everyone gives money to charity. This is called Zakat-ul-Fitr. The idea is that everyone should have enough money to be able to celebrate the festival properly.

On the night that Ramadan ends, many Muslims do not go to bed. They meet friends outside and watch together for the new moon. When it appears, the new month of Shawwal has begun. The festival can begin!

In the past, the beginning of the festival was announced by the muezzin calling the people to prayer from the mosque. Today, it is announced on radio and television. As soon as the festival has officially begun, everyone rushes to greet each other. They wish each other Happy Id by saying, "Id mubarak," and there is much handshaking and hugging. Everyone is in a holiday mood, congratulating each other on completing the fast. People usually break the fast with a light snack. The evening prayers follow, and then the main meal of the day.

On Id day, everyone wears their best (or new) clothes. There are special services at the mosque or place where large numbers of Muslims can meet. These are often the largest congregations of the year, and thousands of people may gather together to celebrate the festival. The main meal is at lunchtime, and it is the best the family can afford. Most people meet with friends or relatives and spend the rest of the day visiting or being visited. Id is a chance for people who have not seen each other for a long time to meet and talk. There are parties, and people exchange presents and cards. In Muslim countries, Id is a three-day holiday.

Id-ul-Adha

Id-ul-Adha takes place in the month of Zulhijjah. It is the most important festival of the Muslim year. It forms part of the Hajj, but it is celebrated by Muslims all over the world.

"Id-ul-Adha" means "Festival of Sacrifice." It is the time when Muslims remember the story in the Qur'an about how Abraham was asked to sacrifice his son, Ishmael, as a test of his submission. He did not have to kill Ishmael—as he was about to make the sacrifice, he was told to sacrifice a ram instead.

However, the point of the story is that Abraham was ready to sacrifice the son whom he loved more than anything because he believed it was what Allah wanted.

The most important part of Id-ul-Adha is sacrificing an animal—a sheep, goat, cow, or camel. It is the duty of a Muslim man to know how to kill an animal so that it does not suffer and the meat from it is halal, or permitted. (In Western countries, slaughtering an animal at home is against the law. It must be done in a slaughterhouse by someone who is specially trained.) The meat from the animal is divided up, and one-third of it is always given to the poor. At the time of the Hajj, the Saudi Ministry of Pilgrimage organizes the disposal and freezing of the carcasses, because there are so many pilgrims that the meat cannot all be eaten at once.

During Id-ul-Adha, pilgrims on Hajj shave their heads.

Zakat

Giving to people who are poor or in need is part of a Muslim's duty. This is called Zakat. Zakat is the third pillar of Islam. Muslims are expected to give 2.5 percent of the assets they received and did not spend on essentials during the year. Zakat-ul-Fitr is the donation to the poor at Id-ul-Fitr, and it amounts to the cost of providing a meal for the whole family. Zakat is not paid openly, so that rich people do not receive false admiration and poor people are not ashamed about receiving it. Giving Zakat reminds Muslims that everything they have comes from Allah and should be used for good.

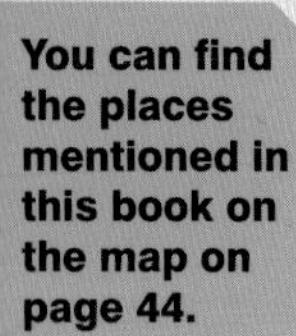
You can find the places mentioned in this book on the map on page 44.

Minor festivals

For Muslims, festivals are not only important occasions for worshiping Allah, but also for improving things that are wrong with people's lives. They are chances to remember the rest of the Muslim family throughout the world and make up for things someone has done wrong or has forgotten to do. Id-ul-Adha and Id-ul-Fitr are the only two major festivals for Muslims, but there are other days during the year that are important.

The Day of the Hijra (Muharram 1)

This is celebrated on Muharram 1, which is the first day of the first month of the year, so it is the Muslim New Year's Day. It remembers the journey that Muhammad made when he traveled to Medina. Muslims regard this event as very important, because it was the beginning of the success of Islam.

In this mosque in Yemen, the stained-glass windows add to the beauty of the building.

Ashura (Muharram 10)

This day was a traditional day of fasting before the time of Muhammad. According to Muslim tradition, it is the day when Noah left the Ark, and when Allah saved Moses from the **pharaoh**. The day is particularly important for Shiite Muslims, who remember the martyrdom of Husain (see page 13).

Mawlid an-Nabi (Rabi al-Awwal 12)

This is Muhammad's birthday, which probably fell on August 20, 570 CE. In many parts of the world, the day is celebrated with processions and meetings or lectures during which events in Muhammad's life can be remembered. In some places there are "birthday parties" for poor or underprivileged children. Some Muslims do not approve of giving so much importance to any human being, even Muhammad, and so do not approve of the celebrations.

Laylat-ul-Mi'raj (Rajab 27)

This is the Night of the Journey. Muslims believe that on this night, Muhammad made a miraculous journey with the angel Gabriel from Mecca to Jerusalem.

They rode on the back of an animal called al-Buraq, meaning "the Lightning," which was like a horse with wings. From Jerusalem, Muhammad was taken to heaven. There, he met and prayed with all the prophets and was taught by Allah. Muslims believe that this was when Allah taught the importance of prayer five times a day. Some Muslims believe that this was a vision rather than that Muhammad was physically transported there. The mosque called the Dome of the Rock is built on the site where Muslims believe this happened.

A 16th-century illustration from Iran shows Muhammad's Night Journey. Notice that the Prophet's face is veiled, because to portray it would be blasphemous, or insulting to Allah.

Laylat-ul-Bara'at (Shabaan 14)

This is the night of the full moon before Ramadan. It is sometimes called the Gateway to Ramadan. For many Muslims it is a night to spend extra time reading the Qur'an and remembering that Muhammad began his preparations for Ramadan on this night.

The revelation on the Night of Power

Muslims believe that the Qur'an itself refers to the night when Muhammad was given the first revelation:

Truly we revealed it on the Night of Determination. . . . Better is the Night of Determination than a thousand months. On [this night] the angels and grace descend by the dispensation of their Lord, for settling all affairs. It is peace until the dawning of the day.
(Sura 97)

Laylat-ul-Qadr (Ramadan 27)

This is the Night of Power, when Muslims remember Muhammad receiving his first revelation of the Qur'an. No one knows exactly when this happened, but it is usually celebrated on the 27th day of Ramadan. Many Muslims spend all night reading the Qur'an and thinking about its importance in their lives. In some places, it is traditional for groups of friends to meet and go to pray in several different mosques during the night.

Family Occasions

A father whispers the adhan into his newborn baby's ear.

Islam teaches that babies are a gift from God. Having a large number of children is regarded as a great blessing. Muslims regard it as a duty of parents to bring their children up to become good Muslims.

When a baby is born, he or she is washed and dressed or wrapped in a shawl. Then, the baby is given to the head of the family, who whispers the adhan—the Call to Prayer—into the baby's right ear. Then, the Command to Worship—the command normally given when the congregation is ready to pray—is said softly into the left ear. Muslims believe that this has two purposes. It welcomes the baby into the family of Islam as soon as he or she is born, and it means that the first word the baby hears is "Allah."

There is a custom of rubbing a tiny piece of sugar or honey on the baby's tongue. This is usually done by the oldest or most respected relative. It is a symbol of the hope that the baby's life will be sweet—that is, that the baby will grow up to be obedient and kind.

Diversity in the Muslim World

Muslims around the world interpret their faith in many different ways. For example, some Muslims believe that there should be no separation between religion and state and that governments must be run in accordance with Islamic law. Other Muslims disagree, believing that it is up to each Muslim to follow God's will without interference by the state. Muslims also apply their faith differently in their daily lives. Some Muslims observe their religious obligations very rigorously. Others may be less observant but still pray occasionally and visit a mosque a few times a year. Others may consider themselves to be part of Muslim culture, but are not at all observant.

Aqiqah

The ceremony called **aqiqah** is held when the baby is seven days old. Friends and relatives come to a feast, and the baby is given his or her name. Choosing a baby's name is seen as one of the important duties of parents. Sometimes a traditional family name is used, while sometimes the name of Muhammad or one of his family members is used. A common choice for boys is one of the 99 names of God, with "Abd" in front of it. "Abd" means "servant of" in Arabic. This is a way of saying that the boy will be Allah's servant all through his life. Names suggesting that the child will be a servant of anything other than Allah are forbidden. It is quite common for the parents to stop using their own name when they have a child and become known as the parents of the child. So, for example, if the child is named Muhammad, the parents would become Abu Muhammad (father of Muhammad) and Umm Muhammad (mother of Muhammad).

At the aqiqah, the baby's head is shaved. The hair that is cut off is weighed, and the value of an equal weight in silver is given to the poor. Even if the baby has been born with very little or no hair, a donation is still given. It often exceeds what the hair actually weighs.

Khitan

If the baby is a boy, he must be circumcised. This means cutting off the foreskin, which is the flap of skin that covers the end of the penis. "**Khitan**" is the Arabic word for circumcision. This may be done at the same time as the aqiqah or, if there is some reason to delay, it can be left until the boy is a few months old. Not having a baby boy circumcised would be considered very neglectful by the parents.

Bismillah

Around the time that a child is four, some Muslims, particularly in India, have a ceremony called **Bismillah**. "Bismillah" means "In the name of Allah," and the ceremony involves the child learning the words that begin all but one of the suras in the Qur'an: "In the name of Allah, the gracious, the merciful."

The child learns how to say each word of the Arabic correctly and is also taught how to pray. Whether or not they have been through a special ceremony, all Muslim children from about the age of four are expected to attend the madrassa at the mosque to learn Arabic and learn about Islam.

Children attend the madrassa to learn more about Islam.

Marriage

In Muslim families, marriage is very important. Few Muslims stay single all their lives. Sexual relationships outside of marriage are forbidden. Marriage is important because it joins two families. For many young Muslim couples, marriages are arranged by their parents. This means that older relatives suggest someone who they feel would be a suitable partner. In Muslim law and in the Hadith, the young person has the right to disagree with the parents' choice. The law forbids forced marriages.

Muslims believe that the best relationships are based on suitability and knowing a person's background. If two people are compatible and suitable for each other, love can follow their marriage. In Western countries, this has caused tension and problems in some families. When Muslim boys and girls grow up seeing friends choosing to go out with people of the opposite sex, they sometimes feel that they want to do the same. Other Muslims are happy for their parents to choose their partner, feeling that they will make a good choice.

Marrying more than one person

At the time of Muhammad, a man could marry as many women as he wanted. The Qur'an changed this, saying that a man should marry no more than four women. Even then, the condition is that all the wives must be treated exactly the same. If a man thinks he cannot do this, he should marry only one. Today, treating many wives the same is generally accepted to be impossible, so most men only marry once. However, some men do marry more than one woman, usually if the first one becomes sick or is unable to have children. In Western countries, it is illegal to marry more than one person at a time.

A bridegroom celebrates at a wedding party.

Other religions

According to Islamic teaching, a child takes the religion of his or her father. For this reason, a Muslim woman may only marry a Muslim man, but a Muslim man may marry a Christian or Jewish woman. These three religions have teachings in common. If a Muslim man wishes to marry a member of any other religion, he can only do so if the woman converts to Islam.

The marriage

A Muslim wedding is a simple occasion. There are readings from the Qur'an, an exchange of **vows** in front of witnesses, and prayers.

The imam may be present, but this is not required. Both partners must sign the nikah (wedding contract). This can include anything that they both want to make a condition of the marriage. However, it cannot include anything that would go against the purpose of marriage. So, for example, it could not include an agreement that they will not live together.

The signing of the nikah may take place months or even years before the couple begin to live together. The wedding party, or **walimah**, takes place when they begin to live together. It usually consists of a meal for friends and relatives. They give presents, usually money. In some countries, the walimah is a huge, expensive party that lasts for days. Muhammad disapproved of this, especially where it causes serious financial hardship for the families.

This Muslim bride is wearing traditional dress.

Divorce

Muhammad described divorce as "the most detestable act that God has permitted." Muslims regard divorce as a last resort. However, Islam teaches that if the marriage has truly failed, there is no point in the couple staying together. Once the divorce is final, an ex-husband has no further responsibility for his wife. Either person is free to marry again after divorce.

Salman's view

Salman is 15 and lives in Melbourne, Australia.

My sister, Aisha, got married last year. Her husband, Rashid, is the son of friends of my parents, so we'd known him for years. The marriage was sort of half arranged, because my father and Rashid's father had thought about it a long time ago, but then when Father asked Aisha who she wanted to marry, she suggested Rashid. They got married in the mosque and there were lots of people there. All the women had spent ages getting food ready for the party afterward, and we had a really good time.

Death and beyond

A funeral is held at Regent's Park Mosque, London.

When a Muslim is near death, friends and relatives gather around his or her bed. The person asks their forgiveness for anything he or she may have done wrong. The person asks forgiveness from God, too. If possible, the last words the dying person says are the Shahadah: "There is no God except Allah, and Muhammad is the messenger of Allah."

Muslims prefer that the body be washed by relatives as soon as possible after death. Then, it may be **anointed** with spices and wrapped in a shroud of white cloth. This may be the ihram cloth from the person's Hajj. People who have died as martyrs are buried unwashed in the clothes in which they were killed, preferably at the place where they died.

Funerals should be as simple as possible. No extravagance is allowed, because death happens to everyone, and it does not matter if the person was rich or poor. Muslims prefer that a body should be carried to the burial ground rather than being placed in a vehicle. It should be placed in a grave in contact with the earth. Coffins should not be used unless there is some reason for them.

Angels

Muslims believe in three kinds of beings: humans, angels, and jinn (spirits). Humans and jinn have free will, but angels must do the will of God. Muslims believe that angels are creatures of light who are in touch with human beings all the time. When someone prays or thinks about God, the angels gather around and join in. Human beings only see angels on very rare occasions, but this does not mean that they are not there. They can take any form they wish. For example, when Muhammad first saw the angel Gabriel, it was as an enormous creature who covered the horizon and had thousands of wings. When Gabriel appeared to Mary to announce the birth of Jesus, it was as a human being.

Muslims believe that every person has two special angels with them all the time. The angels keep a record of everything the person does throughout his or her life. At the Day of Judgment, this is given to the person, who can then figure out what his or her destiny should be. At the end of formal prayers, Muslims turn their heads from side to side to greet these angels.

Muslims prefer a body to be buried with the face turned to the right, facing Mecca. For this reason, they prefer their own burial plots, because those designed for other religions may not allow Muslim graves to be placed in the right direction. Simple headstones may record the name of someone who has died, but Muslims do not believe that it is right for large sums of money to be spent on very ornate memorials.

After death

Muslims believe that when people die, their souls wait for the Day of Judgment. This period of waiting is known as being "in **barzakh**." The Day of Judgment may not happen for hundreds or even thousands of years, but time in barzakh is not the same as time on Earth, and it will pass in a flash. Then, the Day of Judgment—the end of the world—will happen.

Muslim graves face Mecca.

For Muslims, this life on Earth is the shorter part of each human being's existence. It is a test that decides what happens in the next part, after death. If people have persisted in evil ways and refused to acknowledge that they are wrong and ask Allah's forgiveness while they are still alive, it will be too late. There will be no forgiveness at the end of time.

Muslims teach that after the Day of Judgment will come **akhirah** —life after death. Those who have gained Allah's forgiveness will go to Paradise, which is described as a garden of happiness. This will be a state of joy and peace. People who have not believed will go to Hell, a place of burning and torment. Muslims accept that the afterlife is such a totally different dimension that we have no words to describe it.

What It Means to Be a Muslim

In the community

Muslims are very conscious of the worldwide family of Muslims, called the **Ummah**. The fact that people are Muslim is far more important than which country they come from or what color their skin is. This has always been true, but it is probably becoming more so as increasing numbers of Muslims come from non-Arab nations. Although many people, especially in the West, tend to associate Islam with Arabs, at the beginning of the 21st century, only one-sixth of all Muslims are Arab.

Family life is very important to Muslims.

Islam encourages people to be sociable, and meeting friends is very important. Muhammad recommended that you should not go for more than three days without visiting a friend! Guests should be invited to meals wherever possible. Inviting only wealthy people is not approved of. This means that there is always the opportunity to give to the poor. Muhammad once said, "An ignorant person who is generous is nearer to Allah than a person full of prayer who is miserly." Islam teaches that any giving should be done discreetly.

Islam also teaches that both men and women should dress modestly. Muslims believe that wearing clothing that is intended to show off the body is wrong. They feel that it tempts men, which is neither kind nor fair, and is degrading to women. When they are outside the home, many Muslim women dress so that very little of their body can be seen. In some countries women are required to wear a full-length dress and a veil or scarf over their head. This is called **hijab**. Even in places where it is not required, many Muslim women choose to wear it. They feel that it is better to be admired for one's ideas rather than one's body.

For many Muslim women, creating a loving home and family is the most valuable job they could have.

At work

Islam teaches that work is necessary and important. Provided that the job does not conflict with any of the teachings of Islam, what is important is that it is done carefully and well. Although Islam allows a woman to work outside the home, traditionally it is the woman's job to look after the home and the family. The man's job is to provide the means for the woman to be able to do this. Islam teaches that a mother is a priceless treasure, and many women feel that creating a loving home and family is their most important job.

In the home

Respect for other people is an important teaching of Islam. Respect for older people is especially important. They have had more experience of life and so they are wiser and their opinions should be listened to. Parents should be cared for in their old age, because they cared for their children when the children were too young to look after themselves. The concept of special homes where old people can be "put away" is one that many Muslims find difficult to understand.

Shari'ah

"Shari'ah" means "the path." It is the code of behavior for Muslims. Islamic law derives from four sources: the Qur'an, the Sunna, consensus, and analogical reasoning. According to Muslim teaching, actions are divided into five groups. There are actions that must be done, actions that are recommended, actions that are up to a person's conscience, actions that are disapproved of but not forbidden, and actions that are strictly forbidden. Actions in the individual conscience group include most things in everyday life, and people should decide for themselves what to do in the light of the teachings of the Qur'an and of Muhammad. Then, they, like all Muslims, will be able to say, "To Allah we belong and to Him we return" (Sura 2: 156).

Map

The globe on the right shows the location of the map below.

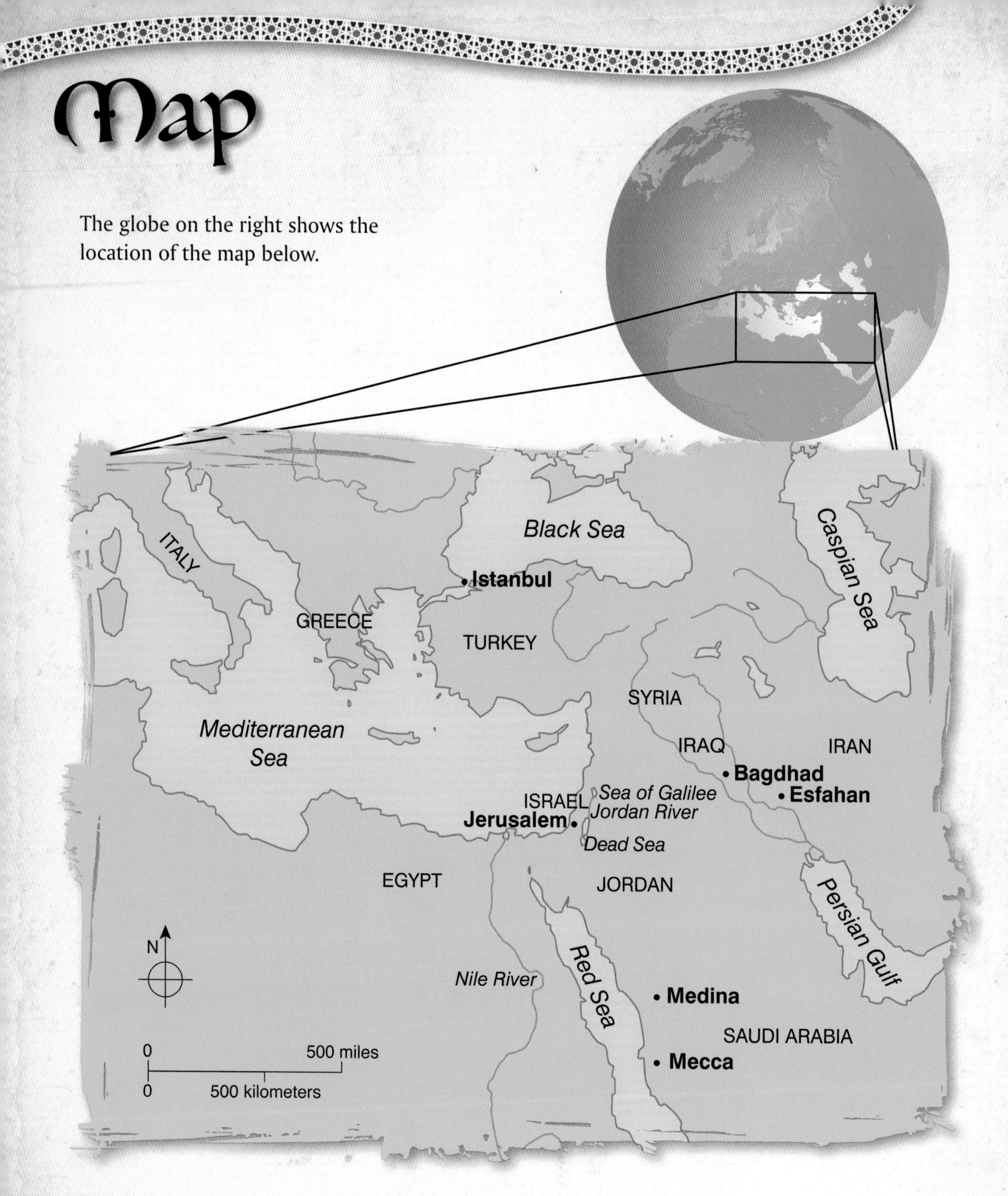

Place names

Some places on this map can be spelled in different ways:

Islaham—Esfahan

Medina—Madinah

Mecca—Makkah

Timeline

Major events in world history

BCE	3000–1700	Indus valley civilization flourishes
	2500	Pyramids in Egypt built
	1800	Stonehenge completed
	1220	Ramses II builds the Temple of Amon (Egypt)
	1000	Nubian Empire (countries around the Nile) begins and lasts until c. 350 CE
	776	First Olympic Games
	450s	Greece is a center of art and literature under Pericles
BCE	336–323	Conquests of Alexander the Great
	300	Mayan civilization begins
	200	Great Wall of China begun
	48	Julius Caesar becomes Roman Emperor
CE	79	Eruption of Vesuvius destroys Pompeii
	161–80	Golden Age of the Roman Empire under Marcus Aurelius
	330	Byzantine Empire begins
	868	First printed book (China)
	c. 1000	Leif Ericson may have discovered America
	1066	Battle of Hastings; Norman conquest of Britain
	1300	Ottoman Empire begins (lasts until 1922)
	1325	Aztec Empire begins (lasts until 1521)
	1400	Black Death kills one person in three throughout China, North Africa, and Europe
	1452	Leonardo da Vinci born
	1492	Christopher Columbus sails to America
	1564	William Shakespeare born
	1620	Pilgrims arrive in what is now Massachusetts
	1648	Taj Mahal built
	1768–71	Captain Cook sails to Australia
	1776	Declaration of Independence
	1859	Charles Darwin publishes *Origin of Species*
	1908	Henry Ford produces the first Model T Ford car
	1914–18	World War I
	1929	Wall Street Crash and the Great Depression
	1939–45	World War II
	1946	First computer invented
	1953	Chemical structure of DNA discovered
	1969	First moon landings
	1981	AIDS virus diagnosed
	1984	Scientists discover a hole in the ozone layer
	1989	Berlin Wall is torn down
	1991	Breakup of the former Soviet Union
	1994	Nelson Mandela becomes president of South Africa
	1997	An adult mammal, Dolly the sheep, is cloned for the first time
	2000	Millennium celebrations take place all over the world
	2000	Terrorist attacks on United States

Major events in Islamic history

CE	570	Birth of Muhammad
	595	Muhammad marries Khadijah
	610	Muhammad receives first revelation from the angel Gabriel
	622	The Hijra ("emigration")—Muhammad's journey to Medina
	624	Battle at Badr between Muhammad's followers and people of Mecca
	625	Battle at Uhud
	628	Treaty made with Meccans
	630	Muhammad claims Mecca for Islam
	632	Muhammad dies
	637	Muslims gain control of Jerusalem
	642	Muslims control Egypt
	644–656	Caliph Uthman ensures that the complete Qur'an is written down
	661–750	Ummayad Caliphate (capital in Damascus)
	681	Husain killed (remembered by Shiites at the Ashura festival)
	690s	Dome of the Rock mosque completed
	711	Muslims conquer Spain
	750–1258	Abbasid Caliphate (capital in Baghdad)
	762–766	Baghdad built (at that time the largest city on earth)
	880	Disappearance of the Mahdi (the Hidden Imam)
	1050–1122	Umar Khayyam (astronomer and Sufi poet)
	1138–1193	Salat ud Din Yusuf (Saladin)—great Muslim soldier and leader
	1332–1406	Ibn Khaldun (great Muslim historian)
	1453	Constantinople is captured by Ottoman forces and renamed Istanbul
	1520–1566	Suleiman the Magnificent (great Muslim leader)
	1526–1857	Mughal Dynasty in India
	1550	Sinan builds Suleimaniye Mosque, Istanbul (considered his finest)
	1571–1629	Abbas I of Iran (established Isfahan as the capital of Iran)
	1616	Blue Mosque in Istanbul begun
	1857	British capture of Delhi ends 1,000 years of Muslim rule in India
	1923–24	The sultanate and caliphate come to an end in Turkey, where Ataturk creates a secular (not religious) "Republic of Turkey"
	1932	Creation of the modern kingdom of Saudi Arabia
	1947	Pakistan created as a Muslim country in the Indian subcontinent
	1948	Israel is founded, leading to further conflict between Israelis and Palestinians
	1953	Enlargement of the Prophet's Mosque in Medina
	1979	Establishment of the Islamic Republic of Iran
	2003	United States invades Iraq, setting off sectarian violence between Sunni and Shiite Muslims

Glossary

adhan	Call to Prayer
akhirah	life after death
Allah	God
anointed	have oil rubbed on the body as a religious act
aqiqah	child-naming ceremony
Arabic	language of Muslim worship and national language in parts of the Middle East and North Africa
Ayatollah	leader of Shiite Muslims
barzakh	period between death and the end of the world
Bismillah	first words of the Qur'an; also a ceremony for children in some Muslim countries
caliph	early leader of Islam
calligraphy	art of beautiful writing
Day of Judgment	end of the world, when Allah will judge everyone
du'a	personal prayers
eternal	lasting forever
fast	go without food and drink for religious reasons
Hadith	teachings of Muhammad
hafiz	title given to someone who has learned the Qur'an by heart
Hajj	pilgrimage to Mecca
hijab	"veil"—used to describe the modest dress worn by Muslim women
Hijra	"departure" or "emigration"—Muhammad's journey to Medina
idol	statue worshiped as a god
ihram	special way of living during a religious pilgrimage; also special clothes that are worn at that time
imam	Muslim leader of prayer. In Shiite Islam, an imam is a leader of the Muslim community who comes from the genealogical line of Muhammad's family.
Islamiat	study of Islam at a mosque school
jihad	struggle against evil to live in the way that Allah wants
Kaaba	most important Muslim shrine in Mecca
khitan	Arabic name for removing the foreskin from the penis
kursi	special stool used to rest the Qur'an on
madrassa	school at the mosque, where students learn the Qur'an

martyrdom	death of someone who dies for what he or she believes
masjid	Arabic name for a Muslim place of worship
meditate	think deeply, especially about spiritual matters
mihrab	arch that shows the direction of Mecca
mimbar	platform in a Muslim place of worship used for preaching
minaret	tower on a Muslim place of worship
mosque	Muslim place of worship
muezzin	man who calls Muslims to prayer
niyyah	intention; also the motive that lies behind an action
Paradise	garden of happiness for life with Allah after death
pharaoh	Egyptian king
pilgrimage	journey for religious reasons
prophet	messenger from God
prostrate	to show submission by kneeling and touching one's forehead to the ground
qiblah	direction of Mecca
Qur'an	Muslim holy book
rak'ah	set of positions for Muslim prayers
Ramadan	ninth month of the Muslim calendar when Muslims fast during daylight hours
retreat	special time of prayer and meditation
revelation	spiritual experience in which something is revealed (for example, Muhammad receiving the Qur'an)
sacrifice	killing something so that its life can be an offering
Salat	prayer
Sawm	fasting
Shahadah	Muslim Declaration of Faith
shrine	holy place
Ummah	worldwide Muslim family
Umrah	religious journey to Mecca at a time other than the last month of the Muslim year
vision	dreamlike religious experience
vow	solemn promise that a person makes that commits him or her to a certain path in life
walimah	wedding party
wuquf	"stand before Allah" while on a major religious pilgrimage
Zakat	giving to charity

Further Information

Barber, Nicky. *Islamic Empires*. Chicago: Raintree, 2006.
Ganeri, Anita. *The Qur'an and Islam*. North Mankato, Minn.: Smart Apple Media, 2004.
King, John. *Iran and the Islamic Revolution*. Chicago: Raintree, 2006.
Teece, Geoff. *Islam*. North Mankato, Minn.: Smart Apple Media, 2004.

Index